LIKE AN OLIVE

TIRZAH GOLDENBERG

LIKE AN OLIVE

VERGE BOOKS / CHICAGO

FOR MY PARENTS

שמע [בתי] מוסר אביך
ואל תטש תורת אמך
כי לוית חן הם לראשך
וענקים לגרגרתיך

[My daughter], listen to the musar of your father
and do not forsake the Torah of your mother;
for they are a graceful wreath upon your head,
a necklace about your throat.

MISHLEI/PROVERBS 1:8-9

The letter צ *(tsadi) entered. (. . .) The blessed Holy One said to her,*
"Turn back, for I intend to split you and transfigure you face-to-face,
but you will arise elsewhere." She left His presence and departed.

THE ZOHAR

When [s]he is still isolated, let the letter
of Tetragrammaton be before [her].

R. YAAKOV YOSEF OF POLLONYE

FRONTISPIECE

The word itself is soft and bookish. *Frontispiece* sounds like that thin protective leaf at the front of some old books, the one you lift to see the frontispiece itself. It looks like *forshpayz,* Yiddish for the first of a repast. Some books let you forerelish the map before entering the village. All lodgings illustrated at the outset, here at the forefront of the book. Whittled down to notables, notables to symbols. Folkways in the foreground of the book. A descendant, having committed a page or pattern of folk wisdom to the heart's genizah, shuts the book, kisses front and back covers of the book, the beloved book (a custom she would keep). A descendant enters enchanted shtetlakh by entering outright the openwork of the book.

COMPOSITE

PROOFTEXTS

I

heirloom tehillim preserve with ciphers
elfin tefillin prefigure by binding remains

anachronism inlay like a tincture
to hand, to head, to heart

here

                              here

              & over Hear

with parchment the Quiet
ly written four

the protean un
spoken folklore, alter

the antiQue at the altar
forget like a master

like an extant
fragment remember

G-d's old signature
or life-breath *be*

extra-biblical by less / furtively interpretive

midrash *fight shy of* / *that kind of* composite prooftext

to read in an extant state / to identify it deveQut

wood floor familiar without furnishing
proof

a dream shokeling
in an ecstatic state of prayer

a bellows a piece of alchemical equipment
a curious tallis missing use

even apprentice is absent
who'd oversee this groundwork into flames

gone to her hermitage below image
groveofmostQuietembellishment

gone to a wood
u n c o n s c i o u s f l o o r o f s u r e a n d f l e e t f o o t e d e v i d e n c e

neither artisan

to note nor what

was left in the anteroom

leaving the rest

peculiar as the word

's permissive dark portion

like idols lodging in the woodcut

peculiar as the wood was nevercut

nights the woodcutter won't sleep / the flutist alights in the treetops days / an eruv round the village the woodfolk make / wine underfoot the wood-folk make woodcuts / a fox afoot where curiouser minhagim have been made / barks past elder sycamore / sees our singular dark furniture awake / rouses antique leathern threadbare bellows / furnishing unwonted flame / barks the route to write the annals / secretly like the Tao / worded like the nigun isn't o / gently heating loophole of the blech / all rabbinic handi-craft is symbol / all symbol's handicraft / all's golden threads in lions em-broidered on dark curtains / the eruv's up, secure / a fox afoot before the ark's dark door / to Torah sing secure / all's arc's dark door to Torah

the letters are plain furnishing

phials for quickening

bellows before hearth

faulty and *likely*

to be all clarity

altering round feeling a while

the Jew the while altering

your yad's yield of literal mistakes

complete with pomegranates

above the decorative

non-figurative

breastplate

archaeologists depend on material culture

all our hopes for something inscribed

the more unprovenanced the better

different from what any one supposed, and luckier

in an earlier era we picked up today's exegetical remarks

emotional about the material of verbal era

(the remains of) anything belonging to the rebels

her sandals near to

her braided hair

olives to alephs

in the hidden press

the earthly

angelic liturgy

figs pressed

to figments

their bones

and their bones

dates to dates

of Shabbos moons

of holy scrolls

our talismans

to sing like the angels

rebels b'yachad

our drawn lots

our fruits

early Hebrew

ostraca

FOR

The virtue of angels is that they cannot deteriorate,
and their flaw is that they cannot improve.

HASIDIC SAYING

a language of lore, of lure, of cleft, of where
    the cleaving angels never cease
        you knowing, continually sing ...

a song of occulted singing, o I'd as lief
    know as not by what earthly means
        my friend ...

my desire is simple
    my dialect antique, but simple
        don't the angels ...

don't the angels with the aid of their hymnals
    don't the angels with their twofold simples
        seem a cure?

when Song of Songs
is the only song

one angels liturgy Ein Sof
tirelessly

in the image of the goats
as it is written in the book

for pages the beloved is
your hands remembering for pages

yourself without a tent
nothing between you and Ein Gedi

endlessly alike, a song
of descending ibex

a hoof-
like liturgy your heart

FOR SASHA STEENSEN

if you'd come
beating upon
my heart
's little door
you'd hear
one little goat
one little goat
my father bought for two zuzim
one little psalm at the tail end of winter
with nothing blowing

between your house
and mine
if one little goat came bleating
wearing as garland one little bell
in time to my running up one little hill
my belly'd be full
or if in a field
even further afield
a cow's choral bell grew near
the sound of herding

somewhere called Awliscombe at night
anywhere called Anycombe at night
where foxgloves
line the hedgerows
in fuchsia hues
where ancient hurts bloom
ecstatic benevolent boon
darkness where fox gloves tread nightly to the coop
where wildness comes wily with
nothing blowing

between your house and mine where

between your house and mine
I climb the highest hill
to say a little prayer
that it echo across the world's wide bowl
to keep you well
where if I'd come
beating upon
your heart
's little door   I
'd leave little

goatbells moving

on the far side

of the dark bushes

seal of the prophet
impression without proof
to imagine—sheer aleph
did anonymous finger impress
an absence or damage the presence
2,700 years ago
the mere suggestion of a grazing doe
aleph like the missing prophet and doe
aleph like half the writing surface
aleph elided—aleph omitted, enriched
with what she is, the diminished mystic
ten feet away from the king

א sheer ל
the letter's belonging
to lack, an identity's profit
ing in clay, א
feeling the rest, the herd
of feeding deer
the mere
א hearing the rest of א

barely did dusk make gift of the feeding deer
but did

               tipped, flooded

the ark made ready
diffuse for gathering One

blessing the clearest yet

altogether cryptic

each etched

toward God toward

the beginning

of the mouth's ritual longing

your mother

your father

anything your eye

opening finds, Theo

the amulet

Theo the secret

sun

O Theo the moon

in the rhythm
of the moon rhythm
moon rhythm of moon
davar never means
merely, o early liturgy
memory's going out in the earliest light
in the *yod* at the *head* breathing *sod*
or Hear what you see
a moon in the mouth of Eudora Welty
a grape from a vine fed from a spoon of silver
sliver of a letter
new moon
to new moon
interims when a Jew
of memory most sound all but pronounces
the holy unpronounceable
fourfold mind
a Quire as it were lunar so
enfolded in my sister
whose name
in translation means
liturgically
o bird of utmost beauty

thus endeth the episode of the ten cent piece
coin's in the minting house
sun's in eclipse
moons since rhymes endeth amulets

FOR MIA RIVKA GUBBAY

Each has an anchor embroidered on her shirt.

GABRIEL LEVIN

the silver thread the Baghdadi thread—the mouth embroiders

anchors & hems Gubbay—the buoy & the bell

lingering in offering the dress alive in the Dead Sea

exhibiting salt's own wedding—cleaving sartorial

to silver sea—tinsel embroidery on silk, lace, late nineteenth century

Baghdad—later altered in London—two Jews meet in a church

unspeaking mouths embroider—unceasing fishing for a glove—another

dropped anchor—finishing something in the pew above—a buoy & a bell

the two in fog—linked—as time to cloth—in mythic cleft—the artist

casts her dybbuk's dark velvet into Sea—to see

salt wed story—ancestry—embroidery—the world is webbed—you said in *silver*

thread Baghdadi thread—the world is wedded—in the occasion of its curation

its duration in mystical salt protect you

on the commune in the silence of a summer's day

my it's hot and still today—a woman's, Meg's, palm opens, offering milk

weed to eat—delicacy in the scales

he's set for a fish—her son, her eldest, supposing his soul guesses

at bottom the lesson is

to eat

      silence, summer's day, *my it's hot*

and still today, at home on the commune, deliberately handmade, mother

tender with water, mother with aloe for their burns allows lions,

harps their laughter, helps their somer

saults in air—Meg laughs—Meg calls the cat—a chrysalis at the stillness

of my window—the sound is singular, the scales are set

I could say, this silent sweltering day—she's airing coos like food for caterpillars

delicacy in the distance from one curious dwelling to the next

On unholy days, at an empty hour, children, apprentices and scribes will fill the tailors' prayerhouse to trace their letters often: what becomes a humble workshop with a few lanterns. Times, a holy thing will happen: the letters'll stop their sound, in scrolls and below bindings, the silence of a stopped up genizah. Children, apprentices and scribes will know the basic elements, knowing weather. Basically, the letter's on the side of silence. It hasn't the wherewithal, with all the strength of the gnarled tree. It has *that kind of beauty which seems to be thrown into relief by poor dress,* and is thus relieved. Times, deep inside the prayerhouse a storehouse quiet enough to be heard hears tailors turning

you haven't the wherewithal

in a kind of folk light.

FOR ANAMIKA JASMINE DUGGER

fluency is less conspicuous

it resembles the secret temple

in every detail

FOR MY MOTHER

women weeping dove code
to one ear, Hebrew
for ancient city, fraught heart

you listen for jackals, a religious
secular silence
is lev's listening jackal

FOR MY FATHER

אבא מדוע

does the Jew expand and contract without end like scribal instruction to
fill a line?

Why does the Jewish Publication
Society's translation
include among the furnishings
for Yahweh's dwelling
the anomalous skins
of the dolphin?

Hayim Nahman Bialik dates the wandering
devotional feeling
to pre-
exilic times—like a rare coin
minted in a rare year
of our revolt
or superfluous oil lamps and vessels. The Hebrew poet
even writes of women
's tribal frontlets resembling tzitzit.

The translation of תחש as porpoise
is based on an Arabic word
which has that meaning. Nineteenth century translators
looked at the Arabic because there was no similar
word in Hebrew or in other
Northwest Semitic languages (to which family
Hebrew belongs).

I'd have worn them, I'd have wrapped scrolls
with my own tribal frontlets resembling tzitzit,

But lately scholars of the Ancient
Near East have pointed
to an apparently cognate word

disappeared or
wandered,
hidden

in ANE languages—duchsu—

a while in a cave

which means

to tell Josephus,

faience ceramic bead,

to be a source.

and have noted ancient references to leather
clothing and sandals with
faience beads. According to this,

Sometimes I imagine I begin
by devotion, question
after question, and sometimes I imagine

the Tabernacle was covered
with leather skins embroidered

I begin from the beginning without end

with faience beads

an historian unfurling

my father embroidering

a fragile bundle

of ancient references

                                    into the poems' purpose

the poems' skins

I.

my goat is found
by the breaking of the vessel
what with the letter is thrown
to psalm
in the palm of the disturbance
of the text, midrashist
only a letter
to seal variance
the image of the secret
on goatskin

II.

where
to,

    sectarian?

to the potter's wheel?
to the purifying waters, the purified set of wares?

to the kosher communal meals?

to the schvitzing sun at Qumran?

to the looms whereon linen and wool never mingle?

to the scribes' lair where they left

us a couple of intact inkpots?

take the Quiet

est byway, never leaving the tel, never neglecting to pocket the least

expensive amulet already to hand, light

on your person, a cave to cup your eyes, say *such adornment*

as may in Tiferet dwell—unitive with mitzvot begin

where hasidim think it good to begin—I, even I—Hashem

winding Her elfin tefillin, composing mitzvot

of Ascent for the Way, bowing to clear

a byway

for Torah in a Quiet room, for fire to adorn

your recently fragmentary hearth unearthed

the Potter's shattered earth ensuring

your wandering amuletic finding, finding

your right hand digging

the earth, listening

how even now you're saying

your listening, encoding

(שמע ישראל ( ) אלהינו ( ) אחד

as if the fringes burst limits

the center burst time

the creaturely sought recitation

in homily and hymn and the rule of blue honey

house of study to house of study

when the esoteric became public it became the center of the heart

fully cosmic

disciples descending to ascend

hills of tekhelet

trails to a courtyard with a trembling flute

piper, wherever

furnishing seems wanting, bring your flute to sound

evolving

the canyon wren reckoning round call it challapeño love dwelling. *Raise it*

again, man. We still believe what we hear.

Bala Cynwyd riddled etrog
hut of the ritual
etmol the middle wood
we past gazelles in spiced hills
besamim

my spine is date palm
my heart citron
from being frum

the moon burst many seals
in the hutted atmosphere
our father in a sweater eating soup

momma pawned a
golden crab she got
from Vedat

I the idling
old bellows sometimes

f   utility
of the heir
loom

may I weave a stranger species
for you both called home

a riddle of the sycamore sefirotic

FOR LEV ALDO KRAJACICH, RECENTLY BORN

like a pomegranate seed on an altar to fertility

engoldened with keter and crowned lev to lev

COMPOSITE
PROOFTEXTS
II

The year [of my birth] was 1918, the first night of Chanukah. The town is Lomza, Poland. I would say half the population was Jewish.

I was born in Darby, PA on October 18, 1892.

My father's name was Gershon. He was in business. The business was leather for shoes. My father, of blessed memory, was president of an orphanage for Jewish children in Lomza. He was also a member of the city council. My mother's name was Gitel.

My mother, Ingeborg Thuv was born in a town in the Lofoten Islands in Norway. The Lofoten Islands are in the Arctic Circle in what is known as the land of the Midnight Sun. For six months of the year the sun doesn't set, and all lamps and candlesticks are put away.

I remember lamps were carried because of the nighttime. We had long hours and we had to walk back from school. We were told two things: Be careful of the lamp, be careful that you don't get involved in any fights with anyone. Come home right away.

My grandfather owned what was called a "station," a place where he sold everything to the fishermen before they sailed on long fishing expeditions. He often went to Russia and other countries for supplies.

My oldest sister was Chaya. In my time, in Lomza, she was married to someone by the name of Pasmanek who had a printing shop, because I re-call that I was asked by my married sister a number of times to carry a hot lunch from our residence to the business, which was about four blocks away.

I must tell you about a little basket he brought my mother. It was heart-shaped and woven out of strips of bright colored glazed paper.

Chaya of course was the oldest. She was already married when I was a kid growing up in Lomza. She had two children. One was born when I was still in Lomza, the other was born when I left Lomza. They were all killed in the Holocaust. Sarah was in America. Leah was the other sister—I grew up with her in Lomza, and she accompanied me on my travels from Lomza to the States. I had a brother by the name of Herman.

For years we would all get together and weave baskets for our Christmas trees. My father filled our baskets with chocolates and each guest who came to see us received one. This is one of my very happy memories.

I remember going to school, which left no deep impression upon me, but I remember the central market, the central market in Lomza, which was let's say a little bit like Machane Yehuda here in Jerusalem, but it was also a bus station at the same time, so I was enamored of all the buses going back and forth.

When they went tobogganing there were eight on the sled and Uncle was always elected to steer it down the mountain and keep it from going over the edge. They would skate for miles on the frozen fjords and all go home for hot chocolate.

I remember my brother-in-law who was killed in the Holocaust was a very nice person, was already somewhat left-oriented, as far as I remember, of those days. He belonged to a trade union. Although he owned a printing shop with one assistant. And I remember that on the Sabbath people walked to shul. I also remember young people, couples, walking hand in hand, young people walking in the public square on the Sabbath afternoon. I always remember the buses.

> My grandmother always hated northern Norway. She was a native of Christiania (now Oslo). She hated the long cold winters and the poverty. We have a hand-made steel darning needle which a woman who had no money gave my grandmother for a little salt.

Otherwise, I have absolutely no memory of Lomza as such, except my parents, our apartment, and of course the Yeshiva of Lomza, which was a famous institution, talmudic institution in that day, in that part of Poland, during that period.

> In those days before typewriters the secretaries and clerks had to stand all day. The hours were long and Mother got in the habit of

leaning on the desk on her left side. It eventually gave her a heart condition. The doctors suggested a sea voyage as being helpful. Mother wanted to go to Australia, but it proved too long to get passage, so my grandmother, Mother and Uncle Fred decided to come to America.

Economic situation in Poland was very, very bad. Sociologically speaking, the anti-Semitism, the hatred against Jews of course was very pronounced in Europe. And America was always the Golden Land, in Yiddish they said the Goldene Medina. Two children were already there, and my grandfather had a hotel and kept saying what are you staying on in Poland for? Why don't you come to America?

Before we leave Norway, I must tell you about my great-grandmother. She lived to be 103 years old. She would take a nap in a large wing-chair. One day she didn't wake up. Wasn't that a wonderful way to live and die?

The quota on immigration was such where only certain people were allowed to come in. That was a little bit traumatic. My parents went first. Leah and I stayed on in Europe [for about two years] with my married sister. It was a bit traumatic because we were in the way of Chaya and her husband, except I was useful by helping out in the print shop. And I missed my parents. But I became very attached to Leah. I became very much attached to her not only because I went with her on the journey, which was already an involved journey—it went from Lomza to Warsaw, from Warsaw to Gdynia, I remember, Gdynia to a German town, from a German town to an English port . . . She was in lieu of my parents, so to speak. She took care of me. Chaya was busy with her husband and with the print shop, etcetera. So she took care of me, I became very much attached to her, so even in the States I was very much attached to her.

My father, Harold S. Djorup, was born May 24, 1861. Grandfather Djorup was a distinguished doctor. He was cited by the King for outstanding work during a cholera epidemic. Denmark has socialized medicine and patients pay by the year. Grandfather's cousin, Pontoppidan, who received the Nobel Prize for Literature, always asked him to read and correct his manuscripts, which he did, and he never wore glasses. He lived to be 94 years old. Several of his sons became doctors, too. The oldest one, Lauritz, inherited his practice. Another one still has his own hospital in Copenhagen. Another one was appointed by the government to practice in a large rural area of Jutland. Some of the daughters married doctors, too. Father became a chemist. And one was the youngest justice of the Supreme Court.

I remember going on the boat and finally arriving in America and meeting my parents and meeting Herman. The question was, where are we going to live, and the answer was very simple. My maternal grandfather was the key situation to all this. He had a very strictly kosher hotel in Lakewood, New Jersey. He was a big scholar, a big talmid chakham, and he was highly respected in the community and even outside of the community. I remember as a kid, when I finally came to the States, national conventions of Orthodox rabbis in those days, the conventions were always held in my grandfather's hotel, which was called the Carmel Hotel located in Lakewood, New Jersey. That part of the family was always in the hotel business in Lakewood, New Jersey. So after a while we moved to Lakewood. I went to a public school, which had a lot of Jewish kids but only one Jewish teacher. They changed my name from Binyamin to Bernard, incidentally, to make me more American. We lived on the wrong side of the tracks. I remember crossing the tracks every day to go to the public school.

> My father was educated in private schools. After the "gymnasium" he, like all gentlemen's sons, was sent on a cruise on a sailing-training ship, where they were taught everything about a ship, even the names of each little piece of rope.

And then they were worried about my Jewish education of course, so they sent me to something called in those days a Talmud Torah, which meant I would go to school after I returned from public school. But my grandfather, being the person he was, a big talmid chakham and always mingled in society of Torah scholars, said to me one day that what I'm getting in Talmud Torah is not enough. He was the one that opened the first Gemara for me. I remember how I sat down with him and learned the first Gemara.

They sailed to the Danish-owned St. Thomas and to Madeira. In Madeira, the thing to do was to buy flowers which the nuns made from feathers. For years Father had a "spray" of a coffee plant. It was made of green, white and red feathers. The nuns are famous for their embroidery. After the cruise he went to the University of Copenhagen and became a chemist. He sailed for America, and on the same ship were my grandmother, Mother, and Uncle Fred.

They sent me away to New York, to go to a place called Yeshiva Torah Vodaas. I lived with an aunt of mine, my father's sister. I stayed with her for a while. I remember having my tonsils removed, eating a lot of ice cream in their apartment, which was very dark, very danky. It was one of those railroad flats on the East Side.

When they arrived in N.Y. he became a chemist for Mr. Edison who invented the electric light bulb. Mother became a governess for the Miller children. Mr. Miller was president of the New York Central Railroad. While there, Mother read an ad in the paper for a chemist at the Pennsylvania Salt Manufacturing Co. in Phila. Father applied and was accepted, and was with them for 45 years. On December 5, 1891, Mother and Father were married in New York. Father gave me the ring for an heirloom.

Again, I'm trying to put together a story which at that point did not make an impact on me, but I can see my father not finding a role for himself in the hotel. He couldn't speak English. He wasn't versed in that business. Of what use is he? The question occurs to me, of what use was he? So I imagine that they were all talking about moving to New York and finding something, living together as a family, as a couple with children, rather than being on someone else's charity or largesse or whatever the case may be. It was after a while that my parents finally made the move, left Lakewood, got an apartment in Williamsburg, my father got a job of sorts, my mother took care of the house, and later on they opened a restaurant in their apartment.

Because of Father's new job, they all moved to Darby, PA. For 12 dollars a month at that time the Reading Railroad ran a train from Darby to a point near the Penn Salt. It was very convenient for Father. When I was one year old they moved to 347 Snyder Avenue in Phila. This was much nearer the Penn Salt, and they sent a carriage for him which they did until he retired (later it was a car).

My father was quiet, soft spoken, and he was somewhat ... the word isn't hurt, but he had traumas of a slight nature coping with the American civilization and the language and the shift from being a businessman, an honorable person who was a member of the city council, and coming to America in the height of the Depression, not being able to find a job, finally finding a job. He had to switch from a world where he was a known businessman to someone working in a factory and traveling by subway back and forth.

When I was two years old, Mother took me to Denmark to be christened, and for Mother to meet Father's family. I was too young to remember any of this. But I was christened by a Bishop who was a member of the family and I was named after my two grandmothers, Anne Augusta Djorup. I had an apple, which the captain of the ship had given me and I said "Peel it" in Danish. I had had all Danish nursemaids and didn't know any English. I have never forgotten my Danish. There is a picture on the table of Mother and me the day I was christened.

The interesting thing about my father, perhaps, was his adjustment to the religious problem in America, when making a living was a very, very difficult thing. Most immigrants were told if you don't come in on the Sabbath, then please don't come in on Sunday, Monday, and Tuesday. You don't have

CENTRAL ATELIERET   AMAGERTORV 10.

a job. And so, many fell by the wayside. The person who had a factory in Pittsfield [Massachusetts], known in Yiddish as a landsman because they came from the same town, offered him a job. He could be Sabbath observant. So he took with him a pot, a potato peeler, and a knife. English he did not know. He gave up his home, gave up everything, being with the family, because he felt so strongly that the Sabbath has to be observed. He's really one of the heroes of that generation of American Jews who stuck with the Torah rather than give it up. I know many people of my age and a little younger who remember that generation in the same sense. When a friend of mine lost his father, and the famous Rav Soloveitchik, who lived in Yerushalayim, the famous Rav Velvele, one of the greatest scholars of our age, came to visit him on the condolence call, he made the following comment which I heard and which really should be enshrined in a book. He said to my friend, "They tell me that in America there are rich Jews. I'm not at all jealous of them. They tell me in America there are Jews who live in palatial residence. I haven't got an ounce of jealousy about them. But they tell me in America there were people like your father who were Sabbath observant and gave up many opportunities in life. Of them I'm very jealous." That was my father living in Pittsfield with a potato peeler and a pot for a number of years.

Mother and Father had many interesting friends. One I particularly remember was a sea captain who stayed at our house every time he docked in Phila. In my button collection I have some nice brass buttons such as he used on his uniforms and which he gave to me. He lost his Danish ship in a storm at sea. He survived, and I met him years later in Denmark. The Peter Tompsens were very good friends. He was a tailor who became a millionaire because of a sailor suit he designed for boys and girls. They were a great success and very fashionable. Mr. Tompsen gave Mother the pattern, even for the escutcheon which was on the arm, and my brother and I wore "Peter Tompsen" suits most of our young lives. Mr. Tompsen kept a yacht in Denmark, his native country. I can still see the very pretty hanging oil lamp in our dining room where we had so many good times.

That's when I met the legendary Mr. Mendlowitz, probably the most influence in my religious life and in terms of community leadership or community involvement. To talk about him requires a volume, and volumes have been written about him. He was never a rosh yeshiva in the understanding of that word. He never lectured on Talmud, although he was a scholar in that area. He taught us Nevi'im, Prophets. He cried when he taught us Chapter 40 in Isaiah. And following that, I learned that big people cry, get emotional about galus, about exile, get emotional about the coming of the Messiah, get emotional about redemption. This was a revelation to me. Then he opened the Siddur and taught us that there's something to be learned from the Siddur itself, not just mumbling words, understand the meaning. Then he would teach us medresh. To this very day I have a love with medresh, I teach a course in medresh. It all came from him. He taught us philosophy as well. He was a very eclectic person. He chose from everything and distilled everything and gave it to us.

One Sunday I was asked to stand before the class and sing—

> Dropping, dropping,
> Dropping, dropping,
> Hear the pennies fall!
> Every one for Jesus,
> He will get them all!

I still have the dainty little cup and saucer I was given as a reward.

Someone told him that I spent Friday afternoons on the East Side browsing in bookstores. Now, you must remember that Williamsburg was separated from Manhattan by a bridge, a river, and it cost three cents to cross the bridge. Well, he was curious to know what do his students do on the East

Side. He called me one day, he says, what do you do on the East Side? I say I go to bookstores. Do you buy? No, because he knew that no one has any money. I don't buy. Browse. He says to me, where do you browse? I mention a name "Vakser," one of the stores. The East Side in those days didn't have so many stores selling electronic appliances and stuff like that. The East Side in those days had bookstores. Loads of bookstores! Not tallesim and stuff like that, but bookstores, religious, non-religious, everything, cultural, for Yiddishists, for Hebraists, there was all kinds of things. Famous, East Broadway and Canal Street. So he asked me. I browse. Where? "Vakser." So he continued with his question. He asked me, what do you look at? I say, well, primarily history books. Which history books? I mention Graetz, Dubnow, I mention a number of things. He says, do you ever look at the history book Yavetz? I said I see it on the shelf, I didn't get around to it. The next Friday he called me over and said to me, do you plan to go to the East Side today? I said I don't know. And he takes out 25 dollars from his pocket, which in those days was a fortune. He says to me, when you go to the East Side I want you to buy for yourself a set of Yavetz's history books, 14 volumes, 25 dollars. You pay me back whenever you think you have the money to pay me back. So I went to the East Side, I bought a set of Yavetz.

מספרי
בנימן גאלדענבערג
—
Ex Libris
RABBI BERNARD GOLDENBERG

Another story, another of the same ilk, the same kind of thing, which I've never made popular, which probably you will not find in books, is the story of Saturday night. One of my very good friends, who didn't go into chinukh, who went into the rabbinate, one of my very close friends ... We all studied philosophy, we studied Tanya, which is the famous Lubavitch handbook. Mr. Mendlowitz, as I said, was eclectic. He taught us Tanya. Since it was the winter nights when he taught us Tanya, so we got through with the class about 7:00, 7:30, etcetera. So some of us left the class, took the elevator train from Williamsburg to Manhattan. Somehow or other they saved up 55 cents. Of course we went to ball games, 55 cents in the bleachers, that's a separate story. (Basically we were interested in baseball, and it was very difficult to go see a ball game, simply we didn't have any money. I mentioned the legendary 55 cents because 55 cents was like crossing the border to Never Never Land, a Wizard of Oz kind of a thing. 55 cents meant we can go to see a ball game at Ebbets Field and hear everything about the players.) But some of us saved up 55 cents and bought a ticket for a play on Broadway which was very popular, written by a guy by the name of Erskine Caldwell called *Tobacco Road*. And these guys just left Mr. Mendlowitz's class in Tanya, went down to Manhattan, Times Square, bought a ticket to watch *Tobacco Road*. Now, my friend Mendel Feldman, the one I was very close with, a very serious human being, the next two Saturday nights— this tells you something about what was going on then, the ferment that was going on in our class—the next two Saturday nights he didn't show up for the Tanya class with Mr. Mendlowitz. I said Mendel, where were you? He says he's learning Tanya. Where are you learning Tanya? At that time there was only one Lubavitcher shaliach in all of Brooklyn, his name was Jacobson, in all of Brooklyn, lived in Brownsville, only one Lubavitcher, before the Rebbe came here! He found him somehow, he found him and he went to his house. Why are you switching from Mr. Mendlowitz in Brooklyn to Jacobson in Brownsville? He says if you can go from a Tanya class to Erskine Caldwell, 55 cents, I can take the subway and go to Jacobson in Brownsville.

It was then that we moved to Merchantville, N.J. I loved it out there. The garden in front of our house had some beautiful shrubs —I especially remember a "bridal wreath" and a "smoke bush." At the back was a *very* large garden. We had eighteen fruit trees and a long grape arbor. Our gardener planted tomatoes and other vegetables. Father used to like to pick a ripe tomato with the dew on it and eat it for breakfast. When Father went on his annual trip to Greenland to put a price on a cargo of cryolite for the Danish government and the Aluminum Co. of America, he was gone for a long time.

I went to Brooklyn College. While in college, going to the evening session after a whole day in yeshiva, you don't have time to be the role of College

Joe, whatever, Joe College, something like that. Anyway, we did some cultural things. I remember, since I was always interested in writing, and had some friends who were already writing for Yiddish papers, and I thought I was well versed in writing Yiddish as well, I wrote a three-column story on Jewish students at Brooklyn College, how they do "Shalom Aleichem," or they sing "Shalom Aleichem," which was partially a lie. I wrote that whole story. And I remember, the great event of my life, I was paid for the column which I wrote, three dollars per column. I made nine dollars when I reported the story about the Shalom Aleichem club in Brooklyn College.

> We would spend endless hours cutting out paper dolls. Marjorie would come to my house or I would go to her house. And we made "pin packs." For this we cut intricate patterns on a square piece of paper. The paper was put in a book and you took a pin and stuck it in the closed pages. This is where the book was opened and the "pin pack" inside was yours to swap.

I got semikhah, I was ordained in '44, '45. And then I became the editor of a magazine published by Agudat Yisrael, called the *Orthodox Tribune*, the forerunner of today's *Jewish Observer*. And so consequently I was very much in touch with the war situation. I initiated a column called "Those Who Fight, Write." Many of the people who didn't go to yeshiva, who left yeshiva, whatever the case may be, it was GIs, and they wrote about the problems. But also we got documents about the war years, etcetera. So we were very much in touch with the situation. The reaction of the Jews was: we don't know too much, we hear what's going on, there's little we can do, Roosevelt is not responding so to speak. But then there were some mass meetings called, and the mass meetings did make an impact on the Jewry, especially the story about the ninety-three girls who swallowed poison rather than go as field prostitutes for the German army. In our circles that created a tremendous thing. Before we knew about the gas chambers, etcetera.

Before we leave Merchantville forever, I must tell you an amusing thing that happened to "Aunty." She had come out to Merchantville to try to get things ready for the movers. She was on the third floor and was all alone in the house when she heard what she thought was footsteps. Every time she moved, there were the footsteps! For once in her life she was terrified. As she started down the steps she discovered that a spool of thread was caught in the bottom of her long skirt.

We saw the sages of our time get into taxis on Shabbos, travel from house to house in Williamsburg and Borough Park raising the money. We were all involved in raising money in those days. We realized the situation, how important it was, pikuach nefesh.

This had been a happy, carefree time. I shall always remember our large playroom that ran across the front of the house. And the nostalgic fragrance of our collection of acorns and other nuts we had found on our walks with Father and Frank. And the onions and bulbs we were trying to grow on the windowsills.

We tried and there was nowhere news. Then we heard from others that the Lomza ghetto was totally liquidated. Nothing ever came up. They were all liquidated. We have the date written down somewhere. They were killed in the ghetto. I use the asarah b'teves yahrzeit for it.

So we moved to a new house in South Philadelphia. Across the street were acres of ground owned by an old Phila family. On this particular piece of land they raised thousands of beautiful peonies which were a joy to all of us, especially my mother.

It was Mr. Mendlowitz's idea that now we know it's a true story of Europe; there's nothing to look forward to in Europe; you got to do something in America. And therefore he pushed for the organization of Torah Umesorah and he took the famous rosh yeshivas and the scholars to head it up. These were the dynamic years when the war was over. There were no day schools except two day schools out of New York. We knew that the GIs were different than the immigrant generation. The immigrant generation was afraid of day schools. They felt that you wouldn't learn any English, you wouldn't get a job. "Make sure you take off your kippah before you go into the office for the interview." That was the immigrant generation.

Because I knew Yiddish and I wrote Yiddish, I worked with him, a full page ad. That ad is a classic, it appears in all the books about Mr. Mendlowitz, the ad saying now is the time to build day schools all over America and outside of New York. It was very powerful. It was printed as a full page ad in the popular Yiddish paper called *Der Morgen Zshurnal* (*The Morning Journal*). This ad did not mention membership nor a dinner nor a contribution nor anything like that, nor a meeting. It merely said why don't you take a look what happened with the Holocaust? Take a look, there's nothing left. What do you want to do in America? There will be nothing left here either. Therefore you have to start building day schools. At the bottom of the ad in very small type—someday I'll show it to you—it says this is a Jew talking to you whose heart is bleeding for the Holocaust and for the fact that we have to do something in America and build day schools.

I, by some strange quirk, which is hashgacha pratis, God's private hashgacha, God's private providence, I wound up in Vancouver [as the Orthodox rabbi of the congregation there], which is a separate story. But we all paid a price, seven years. Why? Because those seven years after the Holocaust, from '45 to '52 when I left, were very dynamic, very stressful, very dynamic. You had to accept the idea of a Jewish education, you had to sell the idea of a Hebrew day school. It was all new. I have stories galore on the strangeness of the Jewish community. "You East Sider you, you Jew you, you New Yorker you, you Communist you, get out of my town!" Orthodoxy as such was not accepted. Everyone felt that Orthodoxy is going out in the 60s. Finished. What's left of Orthodoxy? Here there was a chance with the help of God.

TINY ESSAY
ON QUANTITY

FOR TODD, MEG, LEO, & HARPER

Anonymous, without name: modesty or merely that which *belonged, once, to*, adrift from its source when nothing is. A name would pose a limit; anonymous shies away from limits. In some sense it is perfect, infinite: *perfectly anonymous* coins Gustaf Sobin in his slim, incomplete collection of essays *Aura*, where he left off. Perfectly anonymous, or, a fully developed namelessness: here an artifact, there a bone. Just as a sandal, which out-lasts a foot—*the feet / by spangled straps covered*—is evidence of she who walked with it, so a name—*for Gyrinno*—evidences invisible garments, her *transparent dress*. With less evidence a name suffices for its own dress, a sandal the sole memory of a foot. Such perfection amounts to what is *al-together possible*. The survival of *indiscriminate detail* nonetheless discrim-inates: a remainder is inevitable, somehow prearranged, holding a quan-tity of memory or prophecy. None the less. To prophesy your memory of living injury, as one can read or be read by bone: *for it's the injury alone . . . that serves to perpetuate an individual's signature.*

We live in a tiny house, where it is all too easy to break a dish. Your size does it, thus you practice grace whose virtue is patience. We collect the fragments—what else to perfect them with but gold? The art of *kintsugi* is like the artistry of memory. A gold sealant traces fissures before fragments are given up for accident and discarded. A gold sealant re-imagines the whole and lends a measure of wealth to frugality: waste not, want not. Rather than gold we hold a maxim, which may be the very stuff of gilded thought. *A word, the carver remarked, is like a gold coin to him.*

A tiny house can hold only so much of your library, as too your frugal mind. *Only* so much. A tiny house, while holding a limit, widens to its very brim. It occurs to me that a tiny house is the largest house we've lived in. With little room for excess, whatever fits inside is all there is. *Much* and *little* lose definition. *Only* and *so much* loosen and cohere. A few books, a few spools of thread. All sit on a driftwood shelf my husband made for my odds and ends. Gustaf Sobin in the same slim account remembers a king whose means were grand, excessive. He once gave a gift of *countless quantities of gold threads* to a woman whose name is recorded, but what else do we know of the beneficiary, Sobin asks.

When I read I am guided, gilded, and one book remembers another as if by invisible golden threads. The limit of your library is an embroidery of prophetic memory, as much memoried prophecy. As evidence of *countless quantities of gold threads*—which, Sobin reveals, don't themselves remain (how could they: far too frail), but only an account of them—here are three fragments from my library inside the tiny house, embroidered one upon the other as the aim of a palimpsest is to save paper. When I read I am shoemaker or tailor; words are like gold coins, transparent dress to me:

. . . singing a little song about a man who makes a coat out of an old piece of cloth, then when it's gotten tattered he makes a vest out of the coat, then makes a scarf from the tattered vest, a cap from the tattered scarf, a button from the tattered cap, a nothing at all from the button, and in the end he makes this song out of the nothing at all . . .

Even though the house is as small as ever, it has miraculously grown roomy enough, like the hide of a deer, as it is written in the Book. They all work at one bench, Abbas, Gimpels, Getzels, Godels, the Treitels and the Lippes, sewing golden sandals for the daughters of Zion and lordly boots for the sons. The Messiah himself calls on the little shoemakers and has them take his measure for a pair of silken slippers.

The doorkeeper's feet are seven armlengths long
            five oxhides for his sandals
        ten shoemakers worked on them

Note how each piece grows roomy enough, each a haberdashery with its handmade shelves of notions, each a place of work. Note how *there is only the work.* Gaston Bachelard wrote in *The Poetics of Space* that *values become condensed and enriched in miniature.* A tiny house makes them apparent, expands. Lorine Niedecker wrote: *true value expands / it warms.* She, too, lived without plumbing, cherished her pump and stove, sought her *proper / balance / of water, air / and poetry.* Her means, her meaning. My life has everything to do with my poem. To make believe the two are split is inaccurate. Our friends built this hut from recycled wood. It didn't cost much. They lived in it themselves, then offered its wisdom to us. The overhead is low so we can write, properly balanced with earning our bread. Such perfection amounts to what is altogether possible. *No layoff / from this / condensery.*

Yes, once the tiny house is excepted there's no layoff from what it condenses. Our desires become less and less excessive. Words become precious exceptions, indeed little remains. Gustaf Sobin remembers the scarce light in a medieval household, *the precious exception in the midst of a massed, impacted darkness.* How is it altogether possible that such precious exception would after centuries survive to prove this minimal fact? Iron candlesticks and glass shards of oil lamps have been unearthed, the sanctity of light reimagined: perfectly anonymous minimal light. *On archeological evidence alone, the light it once shed would seem to have been inextinguishable.* As if what is most precious, truly valuable, and as it happens, most scarce, were by such nature the determinant of an indeterminate future. Prophetic light. We light *those tiny little aureoles of radiance*, Chanukah candles near Solstice, to honor the season of darkness and culture.

K'ZAYIT

an excerpt, like an olive, heartily

    but hesitantly pressed

for light of a little learning

    for oil fattening while dim

for oil wisdom, sister

    to a distance, then

disappearance—

    but say the pithy instruction

will alter a person, I

    return to the heart

to the pit

    of an olive-like rabbinics

the miQveh, the river

    precise

immersive

    measurements

Notes

The frontispiece for this book is an excerpt from the Dead Sea Scrolls: the unpronounceable name for God written in ancient Paleo-Hebrew letters, the older form of יהוה. The text that surrounds the Name is written in the contemporaneous Hebrew script. I was enchanted when I first witnessed this unique signature in a museum exhibition of the Scrolls. Enchanted because in Jewish tradition יהוה is already ritually set apart by unsaying it. When a reader encounters these four letters in a sacred text they immediately shape-shift into a pseudonym such as "Adonai," a designation that refers to God but keeps us at a remove from *the Name of all names.* Since יהוה is too holy to pronounce (too holy, even, to write: my writing it out here is a kind of transgression), there is always a gap between itself and ... well, itself. Its nature is to hide in something equivalent to it but not in the least like it. A poet friend reminds me that the singular behavior of יהוה is a lot like the nature of language itself.

A note on pronunciation: The "ch" in all transliterated Hebrew and Aramaic words is not pronounced like the "ch" in English, as in "choice." Rather, it indicates the letter "chet" (ח), which has a soft guttural sound. A "kh" has a similar sound to "ch" in modern Hebrew, but it indicates a different letter, the "khaf" (כ).

FRONTISPIECE

A *genizah* is a storeroom in a synagogue for anything past use bearing Hebrew script, a chamber to keep the literature and ritual objects until proper burial, based on the idea that the name of God cannot be thrown away. Sometimes, as with the Cairo Genizah, the contents build up over centuries. *Shtetlakh* are Eastern European Jewish towns no longer in existence.

Tehillim is the Hebrew title for Psalms. *Tefillin* are small leather boxes with attached straps affixed to one's, traditionally a man's, arm and head during morning prayers; the boxes contain passages from *Shemot*/Exodus and *Devarim*/Deuteronomy written on parchment. The middle of the poem echoes Kate Bush's "Jig of Life": *I put this moment here, I put this moment here, I put this moment . . . over here.*

[I] fight shy of that kind of [thing] is borrowed from one of Lorine Niedecker's letters to Cid Corman: *By the way the U. of Milwaukee asked me to give a poetry reading there but I fight shy of that kind of thing. Devequt* refers to one's cleaving or closeness to God.

Shokeling, from the Yiddish, means swaying in prayer; a *tallis* is a prayer shawl traditionally worn by men.

An *eruv* is a halakhic enclosure that transforms a public area into a so-called private one, allowing religious Jews to carry objects between "public" and "private" domains on *Shabbos*. The meaning of *minhagim* is "customs." A *nigun* is a wordless tune or chant. A *blech* is a metal sheet placed on top of a stove in order to keep food warm on *Shabbos*, when it is forbidden to turn a stove on and off.

Likely to be all clarity is excerpted from Cynthia Ozick's essay "Mrs. Virginia Woolf: A Madwoman and Her Nurse": *The hem of a dress is likely to be all clarity, but the heads escape . . .*

A *yad* is a ritual pointer used for public reading of the Torah scroll; the literal meaning is "hand."

[And to die is] different from what any one supposed, and luckier is a line from Walt Whitman's "Song of Myself."

Shabbos or *Shabbat* is the Jewish Sabbath. *B'yachad* means "together," or "as one."

FOR ELLEN BRINKS

Ein Sof is the kabbalistic name for the aspect of God that is beyond comprehension: "Without End."

FOR SASHA STEENSEN

One little goat my father bought for two zuzim is a verse from "Chad Gadya," a mostly Aramaic song sung on the holiday of Passover. *With nothing blowing // between your house / and mine* is remembered from Lorine Niedecker's "I've been away from poetry." *Goatbells moving on the far side of the dark bushes* descends from Gustaf Sobin's "Transparent Itineraries: 1983."

FOR DAN BEACHY-QUICK

Aleph, א, is the first letter, nearly silent, of the Hebrew alphabet. The poem refers to the "Isaiah seal," a clay impression discovered in recent years which may have belonged to the Prophet Isaiah. What's missing is the Paleo-Hebrew *aleph* that would help to spell, following "Isaiah," the designation of "the Prophet." The seal of King Hezekiah and the seal of Isaiah were found on the same stratigraphic layer ten feet away from each other. The other Hebrew letter in the poem is the *lamed*, ל, which when placed before a personal name can mean "belonging to." It occurred to me after writing the poem that *aleph* and *lamed* beside each other spell El, one of the biblical names for God. Inverted, the letters spell "no."

FOR CAROLINE KNAPP

Diffuse is what Caroline said in relation to something I can't remember on our walk by the rushing river.

FOR SHIFRA ZIPPORAH GOLDENBERG

Davar translates to both "word" and "thing" and has many other meanings, revealing how closely bound word and world are in Judaic thought. *Yod*, י, is the tenth and smallest letter of the Hebrew alphabet and is also the first letter of the Tetragrammaton. *Sod*, pronounced "soad," means "secret."

FOR ANNE AUGUSTA DJORUP

Thus endeth the episode of the ten cent piece is a piece of my maternal great-grandmother's humor and/or sincerity borrowed from a note she wrote to my maternal great-grandfather in apology for borrowing a coin.

FOR MIA RIVKA GUBBAY

Each has an anchor embroidered on her shirt is excerpted from Gabriel Levin's essay "Hezekiah's Tunnel" in *The Dune's Twisted Edge*. *The silver thread the Baghdadi thread* is what Mia said in an e-mail in response to a wedding dress I'd encountered at the Israel Museum in Jerusalem, a dress bearing her family name. The poem alludes also to another garment, a dress submerged in the Dead Sea by Israeli artist Sigalit Landau. In Jewish folklore, a *dybbuk* is a spirit of the dead that attaches itself to a living person.

FOR MEG SCHIEL

My it's hot and still today is dialogue from the 1955 film *Picnic*.

FOR POUYA AHMADI, PETER O'LEARY, AND JOHN TIPTON

That kind of beauty which seems to be thrown into relief by poor dress is unearthed from George Eliot's *Middlemarch. You haven't the wherewithal* are the words of a former landlord.

FOR MY MOTHER

The Hebrew word for "city" is עיר, which in modern Hebrew is something like the phonetic equivalent of "ear." The meaning of *lev* is "heart."

FOR MY FATHER

אבא מדוע, *Aba madua*, "Father, why?" *Tzitzit* are ritual fringes traditionally worn by men. The italicized lines on the right side of the poem are my father's words in response to one of my questions via e-mail. My father is my Encyclopedia Judaica; his knowledge of Judaism is vast, and I often turn to him for clarification.

A *tel* is an archaeological hill formed from multiple dwellings at the same site over an extensive period of time. *Such adornment as may in Tiferet dwell* is borrowed from Norman Finkelstein's *The Adventures of Pascal Wanderlust*. *Mitzvot* are the 613 commandments, or more generally moral deeds. *Hasidim* are members of a Jewish religious sect founded by the Baal Shem Tov in Eastern Europe in the eighteenth century. *Hashem*, literally "the Name," is a common name for God which is intimate in nature. The Hebrew that finishes the poem is the central, centering prayer of Judaism, chanted with one's right hand over one's eyes: *Shema Yisrael Adonai Eloheinu Adonai Echad*. The empty parentheses indicate the unpronounceable Name which is instantly replaced with *Adonai* when chanting the *Shema*. *Adonai* is a sort of placeholder. Its translation, which I dislike, is "my Lord."

FOR JOSHUA ZVI GOLDENBERG

Tekhelet is a valuable blue dye mentioned in the Torah, used for various ritual garments, including the *tzitzit*. According to the Talmud, the dye was extracted from a marine creature, the *chilazon* or murex trunculus. The town of Tzfat, where the poem is set, is painted blue. Tzfat became a center of mystical learning in the sixteenth century, continuing to this day. The graves of the sages there are also painted blue.

FOR RICO OWEN MOORE

I learned the term "challapeño" from the food blog mexicanjewish.com. The poem includes a quote from Seamus Heaney's "The Singer's House."

FOR JOSH & SHIF

An *etrog* is a citron for ritual use on the harvest holiday of *Sukkot*, when a *sukkah* or hut is built just outside the home, within which the citron, date palm, myrtle, and willow are shaken in all directions toward the presence of God. *Etmol* means "yesterday." *Besamim* are fragrant spices breathed in to mark the end of *Shabbos* and the beginning of the new week. The meaning of *frum* is "religious."

FOR LEV ALDO KRAJACICH, RECENTLY BORN

Keter, "crown," is the highest of the ten *sefirot* or divine emanations in the kabbalistic imagination. It is the least knowable of the *sefirot* and the point from which all of the others descend.

COMPOSITE PROOFTEXTS II

This work is composed of the autobiographies of my paternal grandfather (my Saba), Bernard/Binyamin Goldenberg, and my maternal great-grandmother, Anne Augusta Djorup, whom I never knew (I was born the year after she died) and for whom I am named (my middle name is Hannah, after Anne). My Saba's stories are gathered from a taped interview conducted by my mother in Jerusalem in 1996, and my great-grandmother's from a hand-written memoir of twenty pages that does not exceed her childhood, written in 1976 when she was nearly 84 years old. I've inherited the coral necklace my great-grandmother is wearing in the photograph from her christening, and my mother keeps her little button shoes.

I'm hoping that both of my ancestors would have been pleased to have parts of their stories preserved in this form; at one point my grandfather hopes for an anecdote he tells to be "enshrined in a book." My intention is to honor them and their storytelling, and more broadly to honor the two very different sides of my lineage, make a warp and weft of them as they have made of me. My mother converted to Judaism and I grew up in an exclusively Orthodox Jewish context. The cultural influence from her side was less pronounced in my upbringing, but it has been helpful for me to think of my maternal line as the parts that are cut away in a wood-cut, allowing the relief to transmit the ink and convey the image, i.e. Judaism. The cut away parts are an essential aspect of the image, and my hope is that throughout this piece there is a sense of foreground and background continuously shifting places.

Glossary of Saba's Jewish terms: A *shul* is a synagogue. A *talmid chakham* is "a student of a sage," a Torah scholar. The *Gemara* is rabbinical commentary that is based on the Mishnah—both the Mishnah and the Gemara comprise the Talmud. The *Siddur* is the Jewish prayer book. *Medresh*, or *midrash*, is biblical interpretation that moves beyond the literal meaning of the biblical text and is also used to refer to the body of literature encompassing such interpretation. *Tallesim* is the plural of *tallis*, a prayer shawl. *Chinukh* in this context refers specifically to Orthodox Jewish education. A *shaliach* is a person sent out from the Chabad-Lubavitch Hasidic group with the aim of bringing Jews closer to Judaism. *Semikhah* is rabbinical ordination. *Pikuach nefesh* means "watching over a soul" and refers to the principle that one is permitted to transgress any religious law in order to save a person's life. *Asarah b'teves*, the 10th of Tevet, is a fast day on the Jewish calendar remembering the Babylonian siege of Jerusalem and the destruction of the Temple. A *yahrzeit* is the anniversary of a death. A *rosh yeshiva* is the head or principal of a yeshiva, an Orthodox Jewish seminary. A *kippah* is a man's traditional head covering.

the feet / by spangled straps covered ... for Gyrinno ... transparent dress. Fragments of Sappho, translated by Anne Carson.

belonged, once, to ... ; altogether possible ... ; indiscriminate detail ... ; and for it's the injury alone ... that serves to perpetuate an individual's signature. Gustaf Sobin, *Aura.*

A word, the carver remarked, is like a gold coin to him. Isaac Bashevis Singer, "By the Light of Memorial Candles," translated by Martha Glicklich and Elaine Gottlieb.

countless quantities of gold threads ... Gustaf Sobin, *Aura.*

... singing a little song about a man ... Jenny Erpenbeck, *The End of Days,* translated by Susan Bernofsky.

Even though the house is as small as ever ... Isaac Bashevis Singer, "The Little Shoe-makers," translated by Isaac Rosenfeld.

The doorkeeper's feet ... Sapphic fragment, translated by Anne Carson.

... there is only the work ... William Bronk, "Of Poetry."

Niedecker quotations from her *Collected Works.*

Gustaf Sobin quotations, again from *Aura.*

K'ZAYIT

K'zayit, "like an olive," is a rabbinic measurement that defines "eating," such that, for example, eating an olive-like amount of food would require one to say a *berakhah achronah,* or a blessing afterwards. A *miqveh* is a ritual bath.

Acknowledgments

I would like to express my gratitude to the editors of the following journals where a few of these works have appeared in either past or present forms: *Dispatches from the Poetry Wars, Eratio Poetry Journal, Flag + Void, Jacket2, LVNG, Small Po[r]tions, West Branch*, and *X-Peri*. I am especially grateful to Jordan Dunn and Lewis Freedman for gathering the *for* poems into a carefully crafted chapbook, and to Peter O'Leary and John Tipton for homing the whole of this composite prooftext, and to Jeff Clark/Crisis for bringing *Like an Olive* to life.

TIRZAH GOLDENBERG

was raised among sycamore trees and rabbinic laws in Bala Cynwyd, Pennsylvania. She is the author of *Aleph*, poetry partially written from fragments of the Dead Sea Scrolls (Verge Books, 2017) and, with Norman Finkelstein, *Thirty-Six / Two Lives: A Poetic Dialogue* (Dos Madres Press, 2021). She lives on the Olympic Peninsula with her husband Rico Moore and their cat Fennel.